Santa's Favorite
COOKIES

Holiday Peppermint Slices

1 package (18 ounces) refrigerated sugar cookie dough
¼ teaspoon peppermint extract, divided
Red food coloring
Green food coloring

1. Remove dough from wrapper. Divide dough into thirds.

2. Combine ⅓ of dough, ⅛ teaspoon peppermint extract and enough red food coloring to make dough desired shade of red or pink. Knead dough until evenly tinted.

3. Repeat with second ⅓ of dough, remaining ⅛ teaspoon peppermint extract and green food coloring.

4. To assemble, shape each portion of dough into 8-inch log. Place red log beside green log; press together slightly. Place plain log on top. Press logs together to form one tri-colored log; wrap in plastic wrap. Refrigerate 2 hours or overnight.

5. Preheat oven to 350°F.

6. Cut log into ¼-inch-thick slices. Place 2 inches apart on ungreased cookie sheets. Bake 8 to 9 minutes or until set but not browned. Cool 1 minute on cookie sheets. Remove to wire racks to cool completely.   *Makes 2½ dozen cookies*

Gingerbread Kids

2 ripe, small DOLE® Bananas
4 cups all-purpose flour
1½ teaspoons ground ginger
1 teaspoon baking soda
1 teaspoon ground cinnamon
½ cup butter, softened
½ cup packed brown sugar
½ cup dark molasses
   Prepared icing and candies

• Purée bananas in blender. Combine flour, ginger, baking soda and cinnamon. Cream butter and sugar until light and fluffy. Beat in molasses and bananas until blended. Stir in flour mixture with wooden spoon until completely blended. (Dough will be stiff.) Cover; refrigerate 1 hour.

• Preheat oven to 375°F. Divide dough into 4 parts. Roll out each part to ⅛-inch thickness on lightly floured surface. Cut out cookies using small gingerbread people cutters. Use favorite cookie cutters for any smaller amounts of remaining dough.

• Bake on greased cookie sheets 10 to 15 minutes or until just brown around edges. Cool completely on wire racks. Decorate as desired with favorite icing and candies.   *Makes 30 to 35 cookies*

Cashew-Lemon Shortbread Cookies

½ cup roasted cashews
1 cup (2 sticks) butter, softened
½ cup sugar
2 teaspoons lemon extract
1 teaspoon vanilla
2 cups all-purpose flour
  Additional sugar

1. Preheat oven to 325°F. Place cashews in food processor; process until finely ground. Add butter, sugar, lemon extract and vanilla; process until well blended. Add flour; process using on/off pulses until dough is well blended and begins to form a ball.

2. Shape dough into 1½-inch balls; roll in additional sugar. Place about 2 inches apart on ungreased baking sheets; flatten slightly with bottom of glass dipped in sugar.

3. Bake 17 to 19 minutes or just until set and edges are lightly browned. Remove cookies to wire racks to cool completely.

Makes 2 to 2½ dozen cookies

Cashew-Lemon Shortbread Cookies

Chocolate Jingle Gems

½ cup (1 stick) butter, softened

1¼ cups packed light brown sugar

1 teaspoon vanilla

2 eggs

1½ cups all-purpose flour

½ cup unsweetened cocoa powder

½ teaspoon baking powder

¼ teaspoon salt

2 cups red, white and green candy-coated chocolate pieces, divided

1. Preheat oven to 350°F. Lightly grease cookie sheets.

2. Beat butter, brown sugar and vanilla in large bowl with electric mixer at medium speed until creamy. Add eggs one at a time, beating well after each addition. Combine flour, cocoa, baking powder and salt in small bowl. Gradually add flour mixture to butter mixture, beating until well blended. Stir in 1 cup chocolate pieces. Drop dough by rounded teaspoons onto prepared cookie sheets. Press 4 to 5 of remaining chocolate pieces on each mound of dough.

3. Bake about 7 minutes or until set. *Do not overbake.* Cool about 1 minute on cookie sheets. Remove cookies to wire racks to cool completely.

Makes about 4 dozen cookies

Cherry Spice Bars

1 (10-ounce) jar maraschino cherries
1 (18¼-ounce) package spice cake mix
¼ cup butter or margarine, melted
¼ cup firmly packed brown sugar
¼ cup water
2 eggs

Glaze
1 cup confectioners' sugar
1 tablespoon lemon juice
1 to 2 teaspoons milk

Drain maraschino cherries; discard juice or save for another use. Cut cherries in half. Combine dry cake mix, melted butter, brown sugar, water and eggs in a large mixing bowl; mix with a spoon or electric mixer until well combined and smooth. Stir in maraschino cherries. Spread batter into a greased 13×9×2-inch baking pan.

Bake in a preheated 375°F oven 20 to 25 minutes, or until top springs back when lightly touched. Let cool in pan on wire rack.

For the glaze, combine confectioners' sugar and lemon juice; add enough milk to make a thick glaze. Drizzle glaze over cake. Allow glaze to set. Cut into bars. Store up to one week in an airtight container with sheets of waxed paper between each layer of bars.
Makes 2 dozen bars

*Favorite recipe from **Cherry Marketing Institute***

Christmas Ornament Cookies

2¼ cups all-purpose flour
¼ teaspoon salt
1 cup sugar
¾ cup (1½ sticks) butter, softened
1 egg
1 teaspoon vanilla
1 teaspoon almond extract
  Icing (recipe follows)
  Assorted candies and decors

1. Combine flour and salt in medium bowl. Beat sugar and butter in large bowl with electric mixer at medium speed until light and fluffy. Beat in egg, vanilla and almond extract. Gradually add flour mixture, beating until well blended. Divide dough in half; cover and refrigerate 30 minutes or until firm.

2. Preheat oven to 350°F. Working with 1 portion at a time, roll out dough on lightly floured surface to ¼-inch thickness. Cut dough into desired shapes with assorted floured cookie cutters. Place cutouts on ungreased cookie sheets. Using drinking straw or tip of sharp knife, cut hole near top of each cookie to allow for piece of ribbon or string to be inserted for hanger. Bake 10 to 12 minutes or until edges are golden brown. Let cookies stand on cookie sheets 1 minute. Remove to wire racks to cool completely.

3. Prepare Icing; spoon into small resealable plastic food storage bag. Cut off very tiny corner of bag; pipe Icing decoratively on cookies. Decorate with candies as desired. Let stand at room temperature 40 minutes or until set. Thread ribbon through cookie holes to hang as Christmas tree ornaments.   *Makes about 2 dozen cookies*

Icing: Combine 2 cups powdered sugar and 2 tablespoons milk in small bowl; stir until smooth. (Icing will be very thick. If it is too thick, stir in 1 teaspoon additional milk.) Divide into small bowls and tint with food coloring as desired.

Festive Cranberry Cheese Squares

2 cups all-purpose flour

1½ cups oats

1 cup (2 sticks) butter or margarine, softened

¾ cup plus 1 tablespoon firmly packed light brown sugar, divided

1 (8-ounce) package cream cheese, softened

1 (14-ounce) can EAGLE BRAND® Sweetened Condensed Milk (NOT evaporated milk)

¼ cup lemon juice from concentrate

1 (16-ounce) can whole berry cranberry sauce

2 tablespoons cornstarch

1. Preheat oven to 350°F. Grease 13×9-inch baking pan. In large mixing bowl, beat flour, oats, butter and ¾ cup brown sugar until crumbly. Reserve 1½ cups crumb mixture. Press remaining crumb mixture firmly on bottom of prepared pan. Bake 15 minutes or until lightly browned.

2. Meanwhile, in medium mixing bowl, beat cream cheese until fluffy. Gradually beat in EAGLE BRAND® until smooth; stir in lemon juice. Spread over baked crust. In another medium mixing bowl, combine cranberry sauce, cornstarch and remaining 1 tablespoon brown sugar. Spoon over cheese layer. Top with reserved crumb mixture.

3. Bake 45 minutes or until golden. Cool and cut into bars. Store covered in refrigerator.   *Makes 2 to 3 dozen squares*

Tip: Cut into large squares. Serve warm and top with ice cream.

Festive Cranberry Cheese Squares

Coconut Clouds

2⅔ cups flaked coconut, divided
1 package DUNCAN HINES® Moist Deluxe® Classic Yellow
    Cake Mix
1 egg
½ cup vegetable oil
¼ cup water
1 teaspoon almond extract

1. Preheat oven to 350°F. Reserve 1⅓ cups coconut in medium bowl.

2. Combine cake mix, egg, oil, water and almond extract in large bowl. Beat at low speed with electric mixer. Stir in remaining 1⅓ cups coconut. Drop rounded teaspoonful dough into reserved coconut. Roll to cover lightly. Place on ungreased baking sheet. Repeat with remaining dough, placing balls 2 inches apart. Bake at 350°F for 10 to 12 minutes or until light golden brown. Cool 1 minute on baking sheets. Remove to cooling racks. Cool completely. Store in airtight container.   *Makes 3½ dozen cookies*

Tip: To save time when forming dough into balls, use a 1-inch spring-operated cookie scoop. Spring-operated cookie scoops are available at kitchen specialty shops.

Double Chocolate Chewies

1 package DUNCAN HINES® Moist Deluxe® Butter Recipe Fudge Cake Mix

2 eggs

½ cup butter or margarine, melted

1 package (6 ounces) semisweet chocolate chips

1 cup chopped nuts

   Confectioners' sugar (optional)

1. Preheat oven to 350°F. Grease 13×9×2-inch baking pan.

2. Combine cake mix, eggs and melted butter in large bowl. Stir until thoroughly blended. (Mixture will be stiff.) Stir in chocolate chips and nuts. Press mixture evenly into prepared pan. Bake at 350°F for 25 to 30 minutes or until toothpick inserted in center comes out clean. *Do not overbake.* Cool completely. Cut into bars. Dust with confectioners' sugar, if desired.   *Makes 36 bars*

Tip: For a special effect, cut a paper towel into ¼-inch-wide strips. Place strips in diagonal pattern on top of cooled bars before cutting. Place confectioners' sugar in tea strainer. Tap strainer lightly to dust surface with sugar. Carefully remove strips.

Christmas Stained Glass Cookies

Colored hard candy
¾ cup butter or margarine, softened
¾ cup granulated sugar
2 eggs
1 teaspoon vanilla extract
3 cups all-purpose flour
1 teaspoon baking powder
Frosting (optional)
Small decorative candies (optional)

Separate colors of hard candy into resealable plastic freezer bags. Crush with mallet or hammer to equal about ⅓ cup crushed candy; set aside. In mixing bowl, cream butter and sugar. Beat in eggs and vanilla. In another bowl, sift together flour and baking powder. Gradually stir flour mixture into butter mixture until dough is very stiff. Wrap in plastic wrap and chill about 3 hours.

Preheat oven to 375°F. Roll out dough to ⅛-inch thickness on lightly floured surface. Additional flour may be added to dough if necessary. Cut dough using large Christmas cookie cutters. Transfer cutouts to foil-lined baking sheet. Using small Christmas cookie cutter of the same shape as large one, cut out and remove dough from center of each large cutout.* Fill cut out sections with crushed candy. If using cookies as hanging ornaments, make holes at tops of cookies for string with drinking straw or chopstick. Bake 7 to 9 minutes or until cookies are lightly browned and candy is melted. Slide foil off baking sheets. When cool, carefully loosen cookies from foil. Use frosting and candy for additional decorations, if desired.   *Makes about 2½ dozen medium-sized cookies*

For different designs, other cookie cutter shapes can be used to cut out centers of cookies (i.e., small circle and star-shaped cutters can be used to cut out ornament designs on large Christmas tree cookies).

*Favorite recipe from **The Sugar Association, Inc.***

Holiday Thumbprint Cookies

1 package (8 ounces) yellow cake mix
3 tablespoons orange juice
2 teaspoons grated orange peel
½ teaspoon vanilla
5 teaspoons strawberry all-fruit spread
2 tablespoons pecans, chopped

1. Preheat oven to 350°F. Spray baking sheets with nonstick cooking spray.

2. Beat cake mix, orange juice, orange peel and vanilla in medium bowl with electric mixer at medium speed 2 minutes or until mixture is crumbly. Increase speed to medium-high and beat 2 minutes or until smooth dough forms. (Dough will be very sticky.)

3. Coat hands with nonstick cooking spray. Shape dough into 1-inch balls. Place balls 2½ inches apart on prepared baking sheets. Press center of each ball with thumb. Fill each thumbprint with ¼ teaspoon fruit spread. Sprinkle with nuts.

4. Bake 8 to 9 minutes or until cookies are light golden brown and no longer shiny. *Do not overbake.* Remove to wire racks to cool completely.   *Makes about 1½ dozen cookies*

Swedish Spritz

**1 Butter Flavor CRISCO® Stick or 1 cup Butter Flavor
CRISCO® all-vegetable shortening**

1 cup granulated sugar

1 egg

1 tablespoon milk

1 teaspoon almond extract

2 cups all-purpose flour

½ cup finely ground blanched almonds

¼ teaspoon salt

⅛ teaspoon baking powder

Colored sugar crystals (optional)

1. Heat oven to 350°F. Refrigerate ungreased baking sheet. Place sheets of foil on countertop for cooling cookies.

2. Combine 1 cup shortening and granulated sugar in large bowl. Beat at medium speed of electric mixer until well blended. Beat in egg, milk and almond extract.

3. Combine flour, nuts, salt and baking powder. Add gradually to creamed mixture at low speed. Beat until well blended.

4. Fit cookie press or pastry bag with desired disk or tip. Fill with dough. Press dough out onto cold baking sheet, forming cookies about 1½ inches apart. (Refrigerate dough about 5 minutes or until firm enough to hold its shape if it becomes too soft.) Sprinkle with colored sugar, if desired.

5. Bake at 350°F for 8 to 10 minutes or until bottoms are light brown. *Do not overbake.* Cool 2 minutes on baking sheet. Remove cookies to foil to cool completely.   *Makes about 8 dozen cookies*

Mincemeat Oatmeal Cookies

½ **Butter Flavor CRISCO® Stick or ½ cup Butter Flavor CRISCO® all-vegetable shortening plus additional for greasing**

1 cup firmly packed brown sugar

1 egg

1⅓ cups prepared mincemeat

1½ cups all-purpose flour

1 teaspoon baking soda

½ teaspoon salt

1 cup quick oats (not instant or old-fashioned)

½ cup coarsely chopped walnuts

1. Heat oven to 350°F. Grease baking sheet with shortening. Place sheets of foil on countertop for cooling cookies.

2. Combine ½ cup shortening, brown sugar and egg in large bowl. Beat at medium speed of electric mixer until well blended. Beat in mincemeat.

3. Combine flour, baking soda and salt. Mix into creamed mixture at low speed until blended. Stir in oats and nuts with spoon.

4. Drop rounded tablespoonfuls of dough 2 inches apart onto prepared baking sheet.

5. Bake at 350°F for 12 minutes or until set and lightly browned around edges. *Do not overbake.* Cool 2 minutes on baking sheet. Remove cookies to foil to cool completely.

Makes about 5 dozen cookies

Holiday Red Raspberry Chocolate Bars

2½ cups all-purpose flour
  1 cup sugar
  ¾ cup finely chopped pecans
  1 egg, beaten
  1 cup (2 sticks) cold butter or margarine
  1 jar (12 ounces) seedless red raspberry jam
1⅔ cups HERSHEY'S Milk Chocolate Chips, HERSHEY'S
     Semi-Sweet Chocolate Chips, HERSHEY'S Raspberry
     Chips, or HERSHEY'S MINI KISSES® Milk Chocolates

1. Heat oven to 350°F. Grease 13×9×2-inch baking pan.

2. Stir together flour, sugar, pecans and egg in large bowl. Cut in butter with pastry blender or fork until mixture resembles coarse crumbs; set aside 1½ cups crumb mixture. Press remaining crumb mixture on bottom of prepared pan. Stir jam to soften; carefully spread over crumb mixture in pan. Sprinkle with chocolate chips. Crumble reserved crumb mixture evenly over top.

3. Bake 40 to 45 minutes or until lightly browned. Cool completely in pan on wire rack; cut into bars. *Makes 36 bars*

Holiday Red Raspberry
Chocolate Bars

Berlinerkranser (Little Wreaths)

1 Butter Flavor CRISCO® Stick or 1 cup Butter Flavor
  CRISCO® all-vegetable shortening
1 cup confectioners' sugar
2 hard boiled egg yolks, mashed
2 eggs, separated
1 teaspoon vanilla
1 teaspoon almond extract
2¼ cups all-purpose flour
  Green colored sugar crystals
24 red candied cherries, cut into halves

1. Combine 1 cup shortening and confectioners' sugar in large bowl. Beat at medium speed of electric mixer until well blended. Beat in hard boiled egg yolks, uncooked egg yolks, vanilla and almond extract. Beat in flour, ¼ cup at a time, until well blended. Cover and refrigerate 3 hours.

2. Let dough stand at room temperature until it becomes easy to handle.

3. Heat oven to 350°F. Divide dough into 2 equal portions. Cut each portion into 24 equal pieces. Shape each piece of dough into 5-inch-long rope. Form each rope into wreath or loop 1½ inches apart on ungreased cookie sheet, overlapping both ends. Brush each wreath with beaten egg whites; sprinkle with colored sugar crystals. Lightly press cherry piece into top of each wreath.

4. Bake at 350°F for 10 to 12 minutes or until edges are lightly browned. Cool on cookie sheets 3 minutes; transfer to cooling racks to cool completely.   *Makes 4 dozen cookies*

Tip: These wreath-shaped cookies are a Norwegian holiday favorite for the family to bake together.

Berlinerkranser (Little Wreaths)

Acknowledgments

The publisher would like to thank the companies and organizations listed below for the use of their recipes and photographs in this publication.

Cherry Marketing Institute

Crisco is a registered trademark of The J.M. Smucker Company

Dole Food Company, Inc.

Duncan Hines® and Moist Deluxe® are registered trademarks of Pinnacle Foods Corp.

Eagle Brand® Sweetened Condensed Milk

Hershey Foods Corporation

The Sugar Association, Inc.